Foreword

Introduction

This eBook is the EIGHT in the series, and the focus is **Digital Supply Chain Transformation with Industrial Automation.**

In today's fast-evolving industrial landscape, businesses must embrace digital transformation to stay ahead. Digital Supply Chain Transformation with Industrial Automation explores how cutting-edge technologies—such as AI, blockchain, smart warehousing, and automated logistics—are revolutionizing supply chains. From enhancing transparency and real-time tracking to improving agility and predictive capabilities, this book provides a comprehensive guide for manufacturing professionals, supply chain managers, and technology enthusiasts.

About the Author

The Author has more than 30+ years of experience in the field of practical applications of Industrial Automation, IoT, MES, Industry Consulting for Manufacturing Organizations.

"Digital alchemy" is a state that a business can strive to achieve by using its assets and technology to redesign operations and innovate. This can help a business digitally transform itself.

Copyright © 2024 by Digital allchemist

Table of Contents

Table of Contents

1.0 Foundations of Digital Supply Chain Transformation

The transformation of industrial supply chains through digital technologies represents one of the most significant shifts in manufacturing and distribution since the advent of mass production. Today's rapidly evolving business landscape demands a fundamental reimagining of how organizations manage their supply chains, moving from traditional linear models to dynamic, interconnected ecosystems powered by digital technologies.

1.1 Evolution of Industrial Supply Chains

The journey of supply chain management has progressed through several distinct phases. In the early industrial era, supply chains were predominantly local and manually managed, with limited coordination between different stages of the production and distribution process. The mid-20th century saw the emergence of basic automation and computerization, introducing electronic data interchange (EDI) and early enterprise resource planning (ERP) systems.

The 1990s and early 2000s brought the internet revolution, enabling greater connectivity and the rise of e-commerce, which fundamentally changed supply chain dynamics. However, these systems still operated largely in silos, with limited real-time visibility and predictive capabilities. The current phase of evolution, driven by Industry 4.0 technologies, represents a quantum leap in supply chain capabilities, enabling unprecedented levels of integration, automation, and intelligence.

1.2 The Digital Transformation Imperative

Organizations face mounting pressure to digitally transform their supply chains due to several critical factors. Customer expectations have evolved dramatically, demanding faster delivery times, greater transparency, and more personalized products and services. Global competition has intensified, forcing companies to seek new ways to reduce costs, improve efficiency, and increase agility.

The COVID-19 pandemic has further accelerated this transformation, exposing vulnerabilities in traditional supply chain models and highlighting the need for greater resilience and adaptability. Organizations that had already invested in digital capabilities proved more resilient during the crisis, adapting more quickly to disruptions and maintaining better operational continuity.

Industry 4.0 represents the fourth industrial revolution, characterized by the fusion of physical and digital systems. In the context of supply chains, this means creating cyber-physical systems that enable seamless integration between physical operations and digital technologies. Key elements include:

- Smart Manufacturing: Integration of IoT sensors, robotics, and AI to create intelligent production systems
- Connected Assets: Real-time monitoring and optimization of equipment and inventory
- Digital Thread: End-to-end digital connectivity across the supply chain
- Autonomous Systems: Self-organizing and self-optimizing operations
- Predictive Analytics: Advanced forecasting and risk management capabilities

1.4 Key Technologies Driving Change

The digital transformation of supply chains is enabled by a constellation of emerging technologies:

Internet of Things (IoT): Networks of sensors and connected devices that provide real-time data about supply chain operations, asset conditions, and environmental factors.

Artificial Intelligence and Machine Learning: Advanced algorithms that can analyze vast amounts of data to optimize operations, predict maintenance needs, and automate decision-making.

Blockchain: Distributed ledger technology that enables secure, transparent tracking of transactions and assets across the supply chain.

Cloud Computing: Scalable computing resources that enable real-time data processing, analytics, and collaboration across the supply chain network.

Digital Twins: Virtual replicas of physical assets and processes that enable simulation, optimization, and predictive maintenance.

5G Networks: High-speed, low-latency connectivity that enables real-time communication and control of supply chain operations.

1.5 ROI and Business Case Development

Developing a compelling business case for digital supply chain transformation requires a comprehensive assessment of both quantitative and qualitative benefits. Key considerations include:

Financial Metrics:

- Cost reduction through automation and optimization

- Revenue growth through improved customer service

- Working capital optimization

- Return on invested capital (ROIC)

Operational Benefits:

- Improved forecast accuracy

- Reduced inventory levels

- Enhanced throughput

- Lower maintenance costs

- Improved asset utilization

Strategic Advantages:

- Enhanced market responsiveness

- Greater supply chain resilience

- Improved sustainability

- Innovation capabilities

- Competitive differentiation

Use Cases:

1.6 Use Case: Procter & Gamble's Digital Supply Chain Journey

P&G's digital transformation initiative serves as a benchmark for large-scale supply chain digitalization. The company embarked on a comprehensive transformation program in 2018, focusing on end-to-end visibility and intelligent automation.

Key Implementation Elements:

- Creation of control towers for real-time visibility across 100+ manufacturing facilities

- Implementation of AI-driven demand forecasting

- Deployment of autonomous mobile robots in warehouses

- Integration of supplier networks through cloud-based platforms

Results:

- 25% reduction in supply chain costs

- 35% improvement in forecast accuracy

- 50% reduction in order-to-delivery time

- $1.5 billion in annual savings through optimization

Lessons Learned:

- Importance of change management and workforce development

- Need for standardized data architecture

- Value of pilot programs before full-scale deployment

- Critical role of executive sponsorship

1.7 Use Case: BMW's Industry 4.0 Supply Chain Transformation

BMW's transformation focused on creating a fully connected, intelligent supply chain across its global operations, with particular emphasis on its flagship plant in Spartanburg, South Carolina.

Implementation Approach:

- Development of an integrated digital twin platform

- Implementation of AI-powered quality control systems

- Deployment of smart logistics solutions

- Integration of sustainable practices into supply chain operations

Key Technologies:

- IoT sensors for real-time monitoring

- Cloud-based supply chain management platform

- Advanced analytics for predictive maintenance

- Blockchain for parts traceability

Outcomes:

- 15% reduction in production downtimes

- 30% improvement in logistics efficiency

- 20% reduction in quality-related issues

- Enhanced sustainability metrics

Success Factors:

- Strong focus on workforce training and development

- Phased implementation approach

- Close collaboration with technology partners

- Clear governance structure and KPIs

2.0 Smart Manufacturing and Production Systems: A Comprehensive Overview

Smart manufacturing represents a revolutionary transformation in industrial production, where traditional manufacturing processes merge seamlessly with cutting-edge digital technologies. This integration creates an intelligent, interconnected manufacturing environment that fundamentally changes how products are made. Through the strategic implementation of Internet of Things (IoT) devices, artificial intelligence, and cloud computing platforms, manufacturers can now monitor their operations in real-time, predict maintenance needs before failures occur, and enable autonomous decision-making across their production floors.

The drive toward smart manufacturing stems from several compelling factors in today's industrial landscape. Modern consumers increasingly demand customized products, pushing manufacturers to develop more flexible production systems. Simultaneously, intense global competition and rising labor costs are forcing companies to seek new ways to improve operational efficiency and reduce expenses. These pressures, combined with growing environmental concerns, have made the transition to smart manufacturing not just beneficial, but essential for long-term success.

2.1 Connected Factory Architecture: The Foundation of Smart Manufacturing

At the heart of smart manufacturing lies a sophisticated connected factory architecture that serves as its technological backbone. This architecture seamlessly integrates both physical and digital infrastructure components. On the physical side, advanced production equipment works in concert with automated material handling systems, while smart sensors and actuators collect crucial operational data. Industrial robots and collaborative robots (cobots) perform precision tasks alongside human workers, while advanced quality inspection systems ensure product excellence.

The digital infrastructure supporting these physical systems is equally sophisticated. Industrial networks, built on protocols like Ethernet/IP and Profinet, form the communication backbone. Edge computing devices process data near its source, while cloud platforms provide scalable computing resources and storage. This entire ecosystem is protected by robust security infrastructure to safeguard sensitive operational data.

The architecture typically follows a logical four-layer model that ensures smooth data flow and system integration. Beginning at the sensor layer, physical devices collect raw data from the production environment. This information travels through the network layer's communication infrastructure to reach the platform layer, where sophisticated data processing and analytics occur. Finally, the application layer presents actionable insights through user interfaces and control systems.

The Industrial Internet of Things (IIoT) functions as the nervous system of smart manufacturing, creating a comprehensive network of sensors and devices that enable unprecedented levels of data collection and analysis. Successful IIoT implementation requires careful consideration of sensor deployment strategies, ensuring that devices are positioned optimally throughout the facility while accounting for environmental conditions and power requirements.

Data management in an IIoT system presents its own unique challenges and opportunities. The system must handle real-time data collection while incorporating edge processing capabilities to reduce latency and bandwidth requirements. Robust data storage and retention policies ensure that valuable operational insights are preserved while maintaining system performance. Quality assurance procedures and seamless integration with existing systems are essential for maintaining data integrity and usefulness.

Real-time production monitoring provides manufacturers with immediate visibility into their operations, enabling quick responses to changing conditions and potential issues. Modern monitoring systems track a comprehensive range of parameters, from basic production rates and equipment status to complex quality metrics and resource consumption patterns. This data is presented through sophisticated visualization systems, including real-time dashboards and mobile applications, making it accessible to stakeholders at all levels of the organization.

Advanced analytics capabilities transform this raw data into actionable insights. Statistical process control methods identify trends and patterns, while predictive analytics anticipate potential issues before they impact production. Root cause analysis tools help identify the source of problems quickly, while performance optimization algorithms suggest ways to improve efficiency and reduce waste.

Predictive maintenance represents one of the most transformative applications of smart manufacturing technology. By leveraging advanced data analytics and machine learning, manufacturers can now anticipate equipment failures before they occur, dramatically reducing unexpected downtime and maintenance costs. The foundation of these systems lies in comprehensive data collection, where sensors continuously monitor equipment health through various parameters such as vibration, temperature, power consumption, and acoustic signatures.

The analysis of this maintenance data requires sophisticated methods that go far beyond simple threshold monitoring. Machine learning algorithms process historical maintenance records alongside real-time sensor data to identify subtle patterns that might indicate developing problems. These systems become increasingly accurate over time as they learn from each maintenance event, creating a virtuous cycle of improvement. Pattern recognition and anomaly detection algorithms work in concert to distinguish between normal operational variations and genuine indicators of potential failure.

2.5 Quality Control Automation: Ensuring Consistent Excellence

The automation of quality control processes has revolutionized how manufacturers ensure product consistency and excellence. Modern inspection technologies combine multiple approaches to create comprehensive quality assurance systems. Vision systems can detect subtle surface defects at speeds far exceeding human capability, while dimensional measurement tools ensure precise adherence to specifications. Non-destructive testing methods allow for thorough inspection without compromising product integrity, and advanced material analysis ensures that raw materials meet required specifications before entering the production process.

The integration of quality data across the manufacturing process creates a closed-loop system for continuous improvement. Real-time quality monitoring allows for immediate adjustments when variations are detected, while statistical process control methods help identify and eliminate sources of variation. This integrated approach to quality management extends beyond simple defect detection to include sophisticated defect prevention strategies and process optimization techniques.

2.6 The Siemens Digital Factory: A Blueprint for Success

The Siemens Electronic Works facility in Amberg, Germany, stands as a testament to the transformative power of smart manufacturing. This facility has achieved remarkable results through the comprehensive implementation of digital technologies across its entire operation. The foundation of their success lies in the complete digital integration of product lifecycle management, where every aspect of production is monitored, controlled, and optimized through digital systems.

The facility's implementation of digital twin technology represents a particularly innovative approach, creating virtual replicas of physical production systems that enable testing and optimization without disrupting actual production. This capability, combined with their industrial IoT platform and AI-powered quality control systems, has led to extraordinary improvements in performance. The facility maintains a remarkable 99.9% product quality rate while achieving significant reductions in defects and energy consumption.

Tesla's approach to manufacturing represents a bold reimagining of automotive production principles. Their highly automated assembly lines integrate advanced robotics with sophisticated AI-powered process control systems, creating a manufacturing environment that can rapidly adapt to changing production requirements. The company's commitment to vertical integration allows for unprecedented control over the entire manufacturing process, from raw materials to finished vehicles.

What sets Tesla's approach apart is their emphasis on data-driven decision making and continuous process optimization. Every aspect of production generates data that feeds into their analysis systems, enabling real-time adjustments and improvements. This approach has yielded impressive results, with significant reductions in production costs and quality issues while improving overall throughput and energy efficiency.

Critical Success Factors and Future Considerations

The implementation of smart manufacturing systems requires a carefully balanced approach that considers both technical and organizational factors. Leadership commitment proves essential, as successful transformation requires not just financial investment but also a clear vision and long-term perspective. Technical excellence must be maintained through robust architecture and careful attention to system integration and security, while operational efficiency depends on continuous optimization of processes and resources.

Looking toward the future, smart manufacturing continues to evolve with emerging technologies. The integration of extended reality systems promises to transform worker training and maintenance procedures, while advanced AI applications will enable even greater levels of automation and autonomous decision-making. Sustainability considerations are becoming increasingly central to manufacturing strategy, driving innovations in energy efficiency and waste reduction.

The journey toward smart manufacturing represents a fundamental shift in how products are made, requiring significant investment in both technology and organizational change. Success in this transformation depends on careful planning, proper system architecture, and comprehensive implementation strategies that consider both technical requirements and human factors. As manufacturing continues to evolve, organizations must remain adaptable and forward-thinking, ready to embrace new technologies and methodologies while maintaining their commitment to operational excellence and continuous improvement.

3.0 Intelligent Warehousing and Logistics: The Digital Revolution in Supply Chain Management

The landscape of warehousing and logistics has undergone a remarkable transformation in recent years, driven by the powerful convergence of digital technologies. This evolution represents far more than simple automation - it's a fundamental reimagining of how organizations can manage their supply chains with unprecedented precision and efficiency. Through the strategic integration of artificial intelligence, Internet of Things (IoT) technologies, and advanced automation systems, modern warehouses have evolved into highly responsive and adaptive fulfillment centers that can anticipate and meet ever-changing market demands.

3.1 Automated Storage and Retrieval Systems: The Foundation of Modern Warehousing

At the heart of intelligent warehousing lies the sophisticated technology of Automated Storage and Retrieval Systems (AS/RS). These systems serve as the central nervous system of modern warehouses, orchestrating the complex dance of inventory movement with remarkable precision. Modern AS/RS solutions combine high-reaching storage racks and bins with automated cranes and shuttles, creating a symphony of motion that maximizes both storage density and retrieval speed.

What makes these systems truly revolutionary is their ability to optimize space utilization while maintaining rapid access to inventory. Imagine a three-dimensional chess game where every move is calculated to perfection - that's how AS/RS operates, using sophisticated algorithms to determine the optimal placement of items based on factors like frequency of access, size, weight, and order patterns. The system's automated cranes and shuttles move with clockwork precision, guided by advanced control systems that ensure safe and efficient operation.

3.2 Warehouse Management Systems: The Digital Brain

The true power of modern warehousing comes from the seamless integration of Warehouse Management Systems (WMS) with physical automation. These sophisticated software platforms serve as the digital brain of the operation, coordinating everything from inventory management to labor allocation. The WMS doesn't just track where items are stored - it anticipates where they need to be, orchestrating complex movements of goods to optimize order fulfillment.

Integration is key to the success of these systems. Modern WMS platforms communicate seamlessly with enterprise resource planning (ERP) systems, transportation management systems, and customer-facing platforms. This creates a digital thread that follows each item from the moment it enters the warehouse until it reaches its final destination. Real-time data flows through this network, enabling immediate responses to changing conditions and providing valuable insights for continuous improvement.

3.3 The Rise of Autonomous Vehicles and Robots

One of the most visible manifestations of warehouse intelligence comes in the form of Autonomous Guided Vehicles (AGVs) and mobile robots. These mechanical workers represent a quantum leap beyond traditional material handling equipment, combining sophisticated navigation technologies with artificial intelligence to create truly autonomous systems. From automated forklifts that can navigate complex warehouse environments to collaborative robots that work alongside human workers, these systems are transforming how materials move through the facility.

The navigation technologies that guide these systems are equally impressive. Modern AGVs and robots use a combination of LIDAR systems, computer vision, and natural feature navigation to create detailed maps of their environment and plot optimal paths through the warehouse. This advanced perception allows them to adapt to changing conditions in real-time, avoiding obstacles and adjusting their routes as needed to maintain efficient operations.

3.4 Advanced Picking Technologies: Enhancing Human Performance

While automation handles many aspects of warehouse operations, human workers remain essential for complex picking and packing tasks. To optimize these activities, modern warehouses employ sophisticated pick-to-light and voice-directed systems. These technologies serve as a bridge between the digital and physical worlds, guiding workers through their tasks with unprecedented accuracy and efficiency.

Pick-to-light systems use LED indicators and digital displays to guide workers to specific storage locations, while voice-directed systems provide hands-free, eyes-up guidance through wireless headsets. These technologies not only improve accuracy and productivity but also reduce training time and enhance worker ergonomics. The systems provide real-time feedback and performance tracking, enabling continuous improvement while supporting multiple languages to accommodate diverse workforces.

3.5 Smart Packaging and Labeling: The Final Touch

The intelligence of modern warehousing extends to the final stages of order fulfillment through smart packaging and labeling solutions. These systems go far beyond simple identification, incorporating RFID tags, environmental sensors, and sophisticated tracking capabilities. Smart labels can monitor everything from temperature exposure to impact events, ensuring product integrity throughout the supply chain.

3.6 Case Study : Amazon's Revolutionary Approach to Fulfillment

In the rapidly evolving landscape of supply chain management, intelligent warehousing has emerged as a cornerstone of modern logistics operations. Through the lens of industry leaders Amazon and DHL, we can observe how cutting-edge technology is reshaping the future of warehouse operations, setting new standards for efficiency and innovation.

Amazon's fulfillment centers stand as testament to the transformative power of intelligent warehousing technologies. The e-commerce giant has masterfully orchestrated an intricate dance between human workers and robotic systems, creating a symphony of efficiency that has redefined industry expectations. At the heart of their operation lies the Kiva robotics system, working in concert with advanced sorting mechanisms and AI-powered inventory management to create a seamless fulfillment process.

The results speak volumes about the effectiveness of this technological integration. Order processing times have been slashed by half, while storage capacity has seen a remarkable 20% increase. Perhaps most impressive is the near-perfect picking accuracy of 99.9%, a figure that would have seemed unreachable just a decade ago. These improvements haven't come at the expense of operational costs – rather, they've contributed to a 30% reduction in operating expenses.

What sets Amazon's implementation apart is their methodical approach to innovation. Rather than attempting a wholesale transformation overnight, they adopted a phased implementation strategy, understanding that success hinges not just on the technology itself, but on the people who interact with it. Comprehensive training programs and strong change management initiatives ensure that employees are not merely adapted to new systems but are actively engaged in their optimization.

3.7 Case Study : DHL's Smart Warehousing, A Study in Enterprise Transformation

While Amazon's approach showcases the potential of robotics and automation, DHL's implementation of smart warehousing solutions demonstrates how traditional logistics companies can successfully navigate digital transformation. Their technology stack, featuring vision picking systems and collaborative robots, is complemented by a sophisticated network of IoT sensors and digital twin technology, creating a virtual replica of warehouse operations for enhanced decision-making.

DHL's success is reflected in concrete metrics: a 25% increase in productivity, 40% reduction in errors, and a remarkable 35% improvement in training efficiency. These achievements stem from their carefully crafted implementation strategy, which prioritizes pilot programs and regional rollouts before wider deployment. This measured approach allows for thorough technology evaluation and worker training, ensuring sustainable long-term success.

The Infrastructure Backbone of Intelligent Warehousing

The foundation of any successful intelligent warehousing system lies in its infrastructure. High-speed wireless networks with redundant systems ensure uninterrupted operations, while sophisticated power management systems, including uninterruptible power supplies and smart charging stations, keep automated systems running smoothly. The physical infrastructure must be equally robust, with careful attention paid to floor load capacity, clear height requirements, and dock configurations.

Workforce Evolution in the Age of Automation

Despite the emphasis on automation, the human element remains crucial in intelligent warehousing. The modern warehouse worker must possess a broader skill set than ever before, combining technical proficiency with traditional warehousing knowledge. Successful implementations require comprehensive training programs that cover not only system operation but also safety procedures and maintenance protocols.

Change management becomes particularly critical in this context. Organizations must develop clear communication strategies and establish feedback systems that encourage employee engagement and continuous improvement. Equal attention must be paid to safety and ergonomics, with regular risk assessments and health monitoring programs ensuring worker well-being in this technology-enhanced environment.

Future Horizons and Emerging Trends

The future of intelligent warehousing promises even greater advances through the integration of artificial intelligence, augmented reality, and 5G connectivity. Blockchain technology is poised to enhance transparency and traceability, while digital twin applications will provide unprecedented levels of operational insight and control.

Sustainability has also emerged as a key focus area, with organizations implementing energy-efficient systems, sustainable packaging solutions, and green building designs. These initiatives not only reduce environmental impact but often lead to significant cost savings through reduced energy consumption and improved resource utilization.

Measuring Success in the Modern Warehouse

Success in intelligent warehousing can be measured across multiple dimensions. Operational efficiency metrics such as order processing time and pick accuracy provide immediate feedback on system performance. Cost management indicators help organizations track their return on technology investments, while customer service metrics ensure that technological improvements translate into enhanced customer satisfaction.

Conclusion

The implementation of intelligent warehousing solutions represents more than just technological advancement – it's a fundamental reimagining of how warehouses operate. As demonstrated by industry leaders like Amazon and DHL, success requires a careful balance of technology adoption, workforce development, and operational excellence. Organizations that can master this balance while maintaining flexibility and scalability will be well-positioned to thrive in the increasingly competitive logistics landscape.

The journey toward intelligent warehousing is ongoing, with new technologies and methodologies continuing to emerge. However, the fundamental principles remain constant: careful planning, significant investment in both technology and people, and an unwavering commitment to continuous improvement. As we look to the future, it's clear that intelligent warehousing will continue to play a crucial role in shaping the future of global commerce and supply chain management.

4.0 Supply Chain Visibility and Traceability: Creating Transparency in Modern Supply Networks

In today's interconnected world, supply chain visibility and traceability have become essential capabilities that transform how organizations manage their global operations. Think of these systems as a sophisticated radar that provides real-time insights into every aspect of the supply chain - from the location of individual products to their condition and status as they move through complex networks. This visibility isn't just about tracking packages; it's about creating a transparent ecosystem that enables better decision-making, enhances risk management, and ensures compliance with increasingly complex regulations.

4.1 Blockchain Technology: Building Trust Through Transparency

At the forefront of supply chain innovation stands blockchain technology, a revolutionary approach to recording and verifying transactions. Imagine a digital ledger book where every entry is permanently written in ink, shared simultaneously across thousands of computers, and verified by multiple parties. This is how blockchain works in supply chains, creating an immutable record of every transaction and movement.

The power of blockchain in supply chains lies in its ability to create trust through transparency. When a manufacturer records that they've produced a batch of products, this information is instantly shared across the network and can't be altered. Smart contracts - self-executing agreements built into the blockchain - automate many traditional manual processes, from payment releases to compliance verification. This automation not only reduces errors but also accelerates operations while maintaining a perfect audit trail.

4.2 Digital Twins: Creating Virtual Supply Chain Replicas

Digital twin technology represents another quantum leap in supply chain visibility. Imagine having a perfect virtual copy of your entire supply chain that updates in real-time - this is what digital twins provide. These sophisticated virtual models combine 3D modeling systems with data from IoT sensors to create living replicas of physical assets and processes.

The applications of digital twins extend far beyond simple visualization. Organizations can use these virtual environments to simulate different scenarios, optimize processes, and predict maintenance needs before they become critical issues. For instance, a manufacturer might use their digital twin to test how a production line change would impact overall efficiency, or a logistics provider might simulate different routing strategies during peak seasons.

Modern track and trace systems serve as the eyes and ears of the supply chain, providing continuous monitoring of products and materials as they move through the network. These systems combine multiple technologies - RFID for close-range identification, GPS for global tracking, and IoT sensors for condition monitoring - to create a comprehensive view of supply chain movement.

The sophistication of these systems extends beyond simple location tracking. They monitor environmental conditions like temperature and humidity, detect potential tampering, and verify product authenticity. This comprehensive monitoring is particularly crucial for sensitive items like pharmaceuticals or perishable goods, where maintaining specific conditions throughout transport is essential for product safety and quality.

4.4 Supplier Network Integration: Creating Seamless Collaboration

The modern supply chain depends on seamless collaboration between multiple parties, and supplier network integration makes this possible. Think of it as creating a digital ecosystem where all participants - from raw material suppliers to manufacturers to distributors - can share information and coordinate activities in real-time.

This integration goes far beyond traditional EDI systems. Modern supplier networks include sophisticated portals and collaboration platforms that enable real-time visibility into inventory levels, production schedules, and quality metrics. These systems also incorporate performance dashboards and communication tools that facilitate rapid response to changing conditions or potential issues.

4.5 Regulatory Compliance and Documentation: Automating Accountability

In today's complex regulatory environment, maintaining compliance across global supply chains requires sophisticated systems for tracking and documenting every aspect of operations. Modern compliance management systems automate much of this process, ensuring that organizations maintain proper documentation while reducing the risk of non-compliance.

These systems cover multiple areas of compliance, from product safety and environmental regulations to trade compliance and industry-specific standards. They automatically generate and maintain required documentation, create audit trails, and provide early warning of potential compliance issues. This automation not only reduces the risk of non-compliance but also significantly reduces the administrative burden of maintaining regulatory compliance.

Walmart's implementation of blockchain technology for food traceability stands as a landmark example of how advanced visibility solutions can transform supply chain operations. The retail giant recognized that traditional methods of tracking food products from farm to store were simply too slow and inefficient for modern food safety requirements. When a food safety issue arose, it could take days to trace products back to their source – a delay that could have serious consequences for public health.

The solution came in the form of a comprehensive blockchain platform built on Hyperledger Fabric. This system creates an unbroken digital record of every food product's journey, from the moment it leaves the farm until it reaches the store shelf. Every participant in the supply chain – farmers, processors, distributors, and retailers – contributes to this digital record, creating a complete and trustworthy history of each product.

The results of this initiative have been nothing short of revolutionary. What once took seven days to trace now takes just 2.2 seconds – a improvement that transforms how the company can respond to food safety issues. Beyond speed, the system has delivered multiple benefits across the supply chain. Food waste has dropped by 30% as better visibility enables more precise inventory management. Recall management, when necessary, happens 50% faster than before, while compliance costs have decreased by 25%.

Perhaps most importantly, this system has enhanced consumer trust by 35%. Customers can now scan products with their smartphones and instantly see where their food came from, building confidence in the safety and quality of their purchases. This transparency has proven particularly valuable in today's market, where consumers increasingly demand to know the source and journey of their food products.

The collaboration between shipping giant Maersk and IBM to create the TradeLens platform represents another groundbreaking application of blockchain technology in supply chain visibility. Global shipping has traditionally been buried in paperwork – a single container shipment might require hundreds of pages of documents passing through dozens of different parties. This complexity created numerous opportunities for delays, errors, and fraud.

TradeLens transforms this process by digitizing and automating much of the documentation and tracking involved in global shipping. The platform creates a single, trusted source of information that all participants can access in real-time. Shipping lines, port operators, customs authorities, and freight forwarders can all see the same information, updated in real-time, reducing confusion and accelerating processes.

The impact of this digital transformation has been substantial. Transit times have been reduced by 40%, primarily by eliminating documentation delays and streamlining customs clearance processes. Documentation costs have fallen by 20% as paper processes are replaced by digital ones. Perhaps most significantly, customs clearance times have improved by 35%, with the platform's transparent documentation and real-time tracking making it easier for authorities to verify and clear shipments.

Critical Implementation Considerations: Building for Success

The success of supply chain visibility initiatives depends heavily on careful attention to three key areas: technology infrastructure, integration requirements, and performance metrics. Let's examine each of these in detail.

The technology infrastructure must be built to handle massive amounts of data from diverse sources. This requires robust sensor networks for data collection, sophisticated processing systems for analysis, and user-friendly interfaces for accessing information. Think of it as building a digital nervous system – sensors act as nerve endings collecting information, processing systems serve as the brain analyzing this data, and interfaces allow users to respond to this information effectively.

Integration requirements present perhaps the most complex challenge. Modern supply chains involve numerous participants, each with their own systems and processes. Successful visibility solutions must bridge these differences, creating seamless communication between internal systems (like ERP and WMS), external partner systems, and regulatory platforms. This integration must be built on standard protocols and secure APIs to ensure reliable, secure data exchange.

Performance metrics provide the feedback mechanism needed to ensure these systems deliver value. These metrics fall into three categories: visibility metrics (how well can we see what's happening?), traceability metrics (how well can we reconstruct what happened?), and business impact metrics (what value are we creating?). Regular monitoring of these metrics enables continuous improvement and helps justify the significant investment these systems require.

Looking ahead, the future of supply chain visibility will be shaped by emerging technologies like artificial intelligence, 5G networks, and quantum computing. These technologies will enable even more sophisticated tracking and analysis capabilities, leading to increasingly automated and intelligent supply chains. However, success will continue to depend on careful attention to fundamentals: clear planning, strong stakeholder engagement, and a commitment to continuous improvement.

5.0 AI and Advanced Analytics: Transforming Supply Chain Decision-Making

The integration of Artificial Intelligence and Advanced Analytics represents a fundamental shift in how organizations manage their supply chains. Rather than simply reacting to events as they occur, these technologies enable companies to anticipate and prepare for future scenarios with unprecedented accuracy. Picture a supply chain manager with the ability to see around corners – that's what AI and advanced analytics provide, transforming vast amounts of raw data into actionable insights that drive better decision-making.

5.1 Demand Forecasting: The Crystal Ball of Modern Supply Chains

Modern demand forecasting has evolved far beyond simple historical analysis. Today's AI-powered forecasting systems combine multiple sophisticated techniques, from deep learning neural networks to advanced time series analysis, creating predictions that account for countless variables. These systems work much like a master chess player, considering not just the immediate moves but analyzing patterns that extend far into the future.

What makes these modern forecasting systems truly remarkable is their ability to integrate diverse data sources. They don't just look at historical sales data – they consider weather patterns, social media trends, competitive actions, and economic indicators. For instance, a fashion retailer's forecasting system might combine historical sales data with social media sentiment analysis, weather forecasts, and upcoming events to predict demand for specific items in different locations.

The implementation of these systems requires careful attention to data preparation and model selection. Organizations must ensure their data is clean and properly structured, choose appropriate modeling techniques, and establish rigorous validation procedures. Think of it as building a highly sensitive scientific instrument – every component must be precisely calibrated to ensure accurate results.

5.2 Inventory Optimization: The Science of Perfect Balance

AI-driven inventory optimization represents another quantum leap in supply chain management. These sophisticated algorithms work continuously to maintain the perfect balance between having enough stock to meet customer demand and avoiding excess inventory that ties up capital. They're like a skilled tightrope walker, constantly making minute adjustments to maintain perfect balance.

These systems employ multiple types of algorithms, each serving a specific purpose. Multi-echelon optimization algorithms consider the entire supply chain network, while safety stock calculations ensure adequate buffers against uncertainty. Dynamic pricing models adjust prices in real-time based on inventory levels and demand patterns. Together, these algorithms create a comprehensive system that can respond instantly to changing conditions.

5.3 Machine Learning in Supply Chain: The Digital Brain

Machine learning applications have spread throughout the supply chain, touching everything from route optimization to quality prediction. These systems learn from experience, continuously improving their performance as they process more data. Think of them as apprentices who never stop learning, getting better at their tasks with each iteration.

The applications are remarkably diverse. In route optimization, machine learning algorithms consider factors like traffic patterns, weather conditions, and delivery windows to determine the most efficient delivery routes. In quality prediction, they analyze production data to identify potential quality issues before they occur. For maintenance scheduling, they predict equipment failures before they happen, enabling proactive maintenance that prevents costly downtime.

5.4 Decision Support Systems: Augmenting Human Intelligence

Modern decision support systems represent the convergence of all these technologies, creating powerful tools that enhance human decision-making capabilities. These systems don't replace human judgment – they augment it, providing relevant information and analysis that helps managers make better decisions.

Think of these systems as highly skilled advisors who never sleep and can instantly process vast amounts of information. They combine real-time analysis with scenario modeling capabilities, allowing managers to explore the potential consequences of different decisions before committing to a course of action.

Let me continue with the real-world case studies and implementation considerations, maintaining a focus on building a deep understanding of how these technologies create value in practice.

Unilever's implementation of AI-driven demand forecasting provides a masterclass in how global organizations can harness artificial intelligence to transform their operations. The consumer goods giant faced a complex challenge: accurately predicting demand for thousands of products across dozens of markets, each with its unique characteristics and dynamics. Traditional forecasting methods simply couldn't handle this complexity with the required accuracy.

The company's solution involved creating a comprehensive AI ecosystem that integrates multiple technologies. At its heart lies a sophisticated machine learning platform that processes data from countless sources – from point-of-sale systems to weather forecasts to social media trends. This platform runs on a cloud computing infrastructure that provides the necessary processing power while ensuring global accessibility. A network of data lakes stores the vast amounts of information needed to train and operate the system, while specialized analytics engines process this data to generate insights.

The results have been transformative. Forecast accuracy improved by 28%, which might sound like a modest number until you consider the scale of Unilever's operations – even a single percentage point improvement can translate into millions of dollars in savings. Inventory costs fell by 15% as better forecasting enabled more precise inventory management. Perhaps most impressively, stockouts decreased by 30%, meaning products were more consistently available when customers wanted them.

5.6 Case Study : Nike's Journey to Predictive Analytics Excellence

Nike's implementation of predictive analytics for inventory management demonstrates how AI can revolutionize even the most challenging aspects of retail operations. The fashion and sportswear industry is notoriously difficult to predict, with rapidly changing consumer preferences and long lead times for production. Nike's solution was to create a comprehensive analytics system that could sense demand signals early and respond accordingly.

The system combines several sophisticated components. Demand sensing capabilities detect subtle changes in consumer behavior that might indicate shifting preferences. Advanced inventory optimization algorithms determine the optimal distribution of products across Nike's global network of stores and warehouses. Price optimization tools help managers make better decisions about when and how to adjust prices to maximize sales while protecting margins.

The results speak to the power of this approach. Excess inventory – a perpetual challenge in fashion retail – decreased by 35%. Fill rates improved by 25%, meaning more customers found the products they wanted in stock. Perhaps most impressively, full-price sales increased by 15%, indicating that better inventory management led to fewer markdowns and higher profitability.

Critical Implementation Considerations: Building for Success

The success of AI and analytics initiatives depends heavily on three fundamental pillars: data management, technology infrastructure, and performance optimization. Let's examine each of these in detail to understand how organizations can build successful implementations.

Data management serves as the foundation of any AI system. Think of it as the fuel that powers the engine – just as a car won't run properly on contaminated fuel, an AI system won't perform well with poor quality data. Organizations must establish robust processes for ensuring data accuracy, completeness, and consistency. This involves not just cleaning and validating data but also creating systems to maintain data quality over time.

Technology infrastructure provides the engine that turns this data into insights. Organizations need to carefully consider their computing requirements, ensuring they have sufficient processing power and storage capacity to handle their analytics workload. This often involves a combination of cloud resources for flexibility and edge computing for real-time processing. The infrastructure must also include robust integration capabilities to connect various systems and data sources.

Performance optimization represents the ongoing tuning and maintenance needed to ensure these systems continue to deliver value. This includes regular model updates to maintain accuracy, system performance monitoring to ensure efficient operation, and continuous measurement of business impact to justify the investment. Organizations must establish clear metrics for success and regularly track performance against these metrics.

Looking toward the future, organizations must prepare for continuing evolution in this field. Emerging technologies like quantum computing promise to enable even more sophisticated analytics capabilities, while edge computing and 5G networks will enable real-time processing of ever-larger amounts of data. Success will require maintaining flexibility in system architecture while ensuring strong foundations in data management and performance optimization.

The journey to implementing AI and advanced analytics is complex, but the potential rewards are enormous. Organizations that approach this journey with careful planning, strong data management, and a commitment to continuous improvement position themselves to achieve significant competitive advantages in their markets.

6.0 Building Resilient Supply Chains in the Digital Age: A Modern Approach to Risk Management

In today's interconnected global economy, supply chain resilience has evolved from a theoretical concept to a business imperative. As recent global events have demonstrated, organizations must not only anticipate and respond to disruptions but also maintain continuous operations during times of crisis. This transformation has been largely enabled by digital technologies, which provide unprecedented visibility, predictive capabilities, and automated response mechanisms.

6.1 The Foundation of Modern Supply Chain Resilience

Supply chain resilience begins with a comprehensive understanding of potential risks and the ability to detect them early. Modern organizations have moved beyond traditional risk registers to implement sophisticated digital frameworks that combine artificial intelligence with real-time monitoring capabilities. These systems continuously scan for potential disruptions across global supply networks, enabling organizations to identify and assess risks before they materialize into major disruptions.

The evolution of risk assessment frameworks represents a significant leap forward in supply chain management. These frameworks now integrate traditional methodologies with advanced digital capabilities, creating a dynamic approach to risk management. AI-powered risk scanning systems work alongside predictive analytics to provide real-time monitoring and automated assessments, while sophisticated scenario modeling tools enable organizations to simulate potential impacts and evaluate different response strategies.

6.2 Disruption Detection: From Reactive to Proactive

The implementation of advanced disruption management systems has fundamentally changed how organizations approach supply chain risks. These systems leverage pattern recognition and anomaly detection capabilities to identify potential disruptions before they occur. Real-time monitoring through sensor networks and analytics engines enables organizations to detect subtle changes in supply chain performance that might indicate emerging problems.

When disruptions are detected, automated response mechanisms spring into action. These systems generate alerts, initiate response protocols, and begin allocating resources according to predefined strategies. The integration of communication platforms ensures that all stakeholders receive timely information and can coordinate their responses effectively.

6.3 Alternative Sourcing: A Strategic Imperative

Digital transformation has revolutionized sourcing strategies, enabling organizations to maintain flexible and resilient supply networks. Modern sourcing approaches emphasize supplier diversification and geographic distribution, supported by sophisticated digital tools for supplier assessment and management. These systems maintain comprehensive supplier databases, integrate market intelligence, and provide real-time cost analysis capabilities.

The implementation of these strategies requires robust data integration and analysis capabilities, coupled with automated workflow systems for supplier onboarding and management. Performance metrics track supplier reliability and compliance, while contract management systems ensure that relationships remain aligned with organizational objectives.

6.4 Business Continuity in the Digital Age

The digital enhancement of business continuity planning has transformed how organizations prepare for and respond to disruptions. Modern continuity plans leverage automated updates and real-time monitoring systems to maintain current and effective response strategies. Scenario simulation capabilities enable organizations to test and refine their plans regularly, while resource tracking systems ensure that necessary assets are always available when needed.

6.5 Crisis Management: The Power of Automation

The automation of crisis management represents a significant advancement in supply chain resilience. Modern systems combine detection capabilities with automated response protocols, enabling organizations to react swiftly and effectively to emerging crises. These systems manage everything from initial alert generation to resource allocation and performance monitoring, ensuring a coordinated and effective response to any disruption.

Toyota's response to the 2011 tsunami provides a compelling example of effective supply chain resilience. Through comprehensive supply chain mapping and sophisticated risk assessment systems, Toyota achieved remarkable results: a 60% faster recovery time and a 40% reduction in disruption impact. Their digital implementation, featuring real-time monitoring and supply network visibility systems, enabled them to maintain operations despite severe disruptions to their supplier network.

6.7 Case Study:Nestlé's COVID-19 Response: Adaptation at Scale

Nestlé's response to the COVID-19 pandemic demonstrates the power of modern resilience capabilities. Their implementation of digital control towers and AI-powered analytics enabled them to achieve a 45% reduction in disruption impact and 30% improved visibility across their supply network. Their success underscores the importance of digital readiness and network visibility in managing large-scale disruptions.

Building Blocks of Implementation

The successful implementation of supply chain resilience requires attention to three key areas: technology infrastructure, organizational requirements, and performance metrics. The technology infrastructure must include robust monitoring systems, communication platforms, and analysis capabilities. Organizational requirements encompass governance structures, training programs, and change management initiatives. Performance metrics track response effectiveness, system performance, and business impact.

Looking to the Future

The future of supply chain resilience will be shaped by continuing technological evolution, including advances in artificial intelligence, Internet of Things expansion, and blockchain adoption. However, success will depend not only on technology but also on organizational readiness and leadership commitment. Organizations must balance the need for enhanced resilience with practical considerations such as cost, complexity, and user adoption.

Conclusion

Building resilient supply chains in the digital age requires a comprehensive approach that combines technological sophistication with organizational readiness. Success depends on careful planning, strong stakeholder engagement, and a commitment to continuous improvement. As global supply chains continue to face new challenges, organizations that invest in resilience capabilities will be best positioned to thrive in an increasingly uncertain business environment.

The journey toward supply chain resilience is ongoing, but the path forward is clear: organizations must embrace digital transformation while maintaining focus on the fundamental principles of risk management and operational excellence. Those that succeed in this transformation will not only survive disruptions but emerge stronger, more competitive, and better prepared for future challenges.

7.0 Digital Supply Chain Integration: Bridging Past and Future in Modern Business

In the evolving landscape of supply chain management, successful digital transformation requires more than just implementing new technologies—it demands a holistic approach that harmoniously blends technical innovation with organizational change. As businesses navigate this complex journey, understanding the intricate dance between legacy systems and modern solutions becomes crucial for sustainable success.

7.1 The Foundation of Successful Integration

At its core, digital supply chain transformation rests on three fundamental pillars: strategic alignment with business objectives, robust architecture design, and effective change management. These elements work together to create a framework that not only enables technical implementation but also ensures sustainable value creation. Organizations must approach this transformation as a comprehensive journey rather than a series of isolated technical upgrades.

Consider how modern businesses operate: they often maintain decades-old systems that handle critical operations alongside cutting-edge digital solutions. This reality creates a unique challenge: how do we bridge the gap between established processes and innovative technologies without disrupting daily operations?

7.2 Legacy Systems: The Art of Modern Integration

The integration of legacy systems presents one of the most significant challenges in digital transformation. These systems, often the backbone of established businesses, cannot simply be replaced overnight. Instead, organizations must carefully orchestrate their modernization through sophisticated integration methods.

Modern integration approaches leverage API development and middleware solutions to create seamless connections between old and new systems. Think of this process as building bridges between islands of information—each bridge must be carefully engineered to handle the specific traffic patterns and load requirements of the data flowing across it.

For example, when a traditional inventory management system needs to communicate with a modern AI-powered demand forecasting platform, data transformation services act as interpreters, ensuring both systems speak the same language. This integration requires careful attention to system compatibility, data format standardization, and performance optimization.

The emergence of cloud and edge computing has revolutionized how organizations approach digital supply chain infrastructure. Cloud computing provides the scalable foundation necessary for modern supply chain operations, offering flexible infrastructure services, robust platform capabilities, and sophisticated analytics engines.

Edge computing complements cloud services by enabling real-time processing and decision-making closer to the point of action. Imagine a manufacturing facility where sensors continuously monitor equipment performance—edge computing allows for immediate analysis and response to potential issues, while cloud systems handle longer-term data storage and advanced analytics.

7.4 Securing the Digital Supply Chain

In our interconnected world, cybersecurity has become a critical component of supply chain integration. Organizations must implement comprehensive security frameworks that protect not only their own operations but also the entire supply chain ecosystem. This protection extends beyond traditional security measures to encompass modern threats and vulnerabilities.

The security framework must address multiple layers of protection, from basic access control and data encryption to sophisticated intrusion detection systems and incident response procedures. Think of it as building a medieval castle with modern security technology—multiple layers of defense working together to protect valuable assets.

7.5 The Human Element: Change Management and Training

Perhaps the most crucial aspect of successful integration lies in managing the human element of digital transformation. The most sophisticated technical solutions will fail without proper change management and comprehensive training programs. Organizations must invest in developing their workforce's capabilities to match the evolving technical landscape.

Effective change management begins with stakeholder analysis and communication planning, ensuring that everyone understands not just what is changing, but why it matters to them. Training programs must go beyond simple system operation to include process knowledge, security awareness, and continuous learning opportunities.

Bosch's digital transformation journey provides valuable insights into successful large-scale integration. Their cloud-first approach achieved remarkable results: a 40% reduction in costs, 35% improvement in efficiency, and 30% faster processing times. Their success stemmed from a carefully orchestrated combination of technical excellence and organizational change management.

7.7 Case Study Johnson & Johnson's Legacy Modernization

Johnson & Johnson's system modernization project demonstrates how established companies can successfully transform their operations while maintaining business continuity. Their phased approach to integration, focusing on risk mitigation and continuous improvement, led to significant achievements: 35% improved system efficiency, 40% better integration, and 45% enhanced security.

Looking to the Future

As we look ahead, several key trends will shape the future of supply chain integration:

The continued evolution of cloud technology will enable even more sophisticated integration capabilities, while edge computing will become increasingly important for real-time operations. Security requirements will continue to evolve, driven by new threats and regulatory demands. Organizations must prepare for these changes while maintaining focus on their current transformation initiatives.

The Path to Successful Implementation

Success in digital supply chain integration requires attention to several critical factors:

Strong leadership commitment provides the foundation for successful transformation, ensuring adequate resource allocation and maintaining focus on strategic objectives. Technical enablement through careful architecture design and integration methodology ensures sustainable solutions. Organizational readiness, developed through comprehensive training and change management programs, enables effective adoption of new capabilities.

Conclusion

The journey of digital supply chain integration represents a complex but necessary evolution in modern business operations. Success requires a delicate balance of technical expertise, organizational change management, and continuous improvement. Organizations that master this balance will be well-positioned to thrive in an increasingly digital business environment.

As we continue to witness rapid technological advancement, the key to successful integration lies not just in implementing new technologies, but in creating sustainable, adaptable systems that can evolve with changing business needs. This requires ongoing commitment to excellence in both technical implementation and organizational development, ensuring that digital transformation creates lasting value for the organization and its stakeholders.

8.0 The Future of Digital Supply Chains: Industry Transformations and Emerging Technologies

The digital transformation of supply chains represents one of the most significant business evolutions of our time. As we examine the landscape across different industries, we see how digital technologies are not just improving existing processes but fundamentally reimagining how supply chains operate. Through detailed analysis of industry-specific implementations and emerging trends, we can better understand both the current state and future direction of digital supply chains.

8.1 Manufacturing's Digital Revolution

The manufacturing sector stands at the forefront of digital supply chain innovation, where the convergence of physical and digital systems is creating unprecedented opportunities for optimization and efficiency. Smart manufacturing systems have evolved from simple automation to sophisticated, AI-driven operations that can predict, adapt, and optimize in real-time.

Consider a modern automotive manufacturing plant: sensors throughout the facility continuously monitor everything from equipment performance to environmental conditions. These sensors feed data into advanced analytics systems that can predict maintenance needs before failures occur, automatically adjust production parameters for optimal quality, and coordinate with suppliers to ensure just-in-time delivery of components.

The implementation of digital twin technology has proven particularly transformative. These virtual replicas of physical manufacturing operations enable companies to simulate changes and optimize processes without disrupting actual production. For example, a leading aerospace manufacturer used digital twin technology to reduce production line changeover times by 25% and improve overall equipment effectiveness by 20%.

Success in manufacturing implementations has consistently highlighted several critical factors:

First, the importance of data quality cannot be overstated. Manufacturing operations generate enormous amounts of data, but this data must be accurate, timely, and properly integrated to drive value. Companies that invest in robust data management infrastructures consistently achieve better results from their digital initiatives.

Second, successful implementations require significant attention to workforce development. The transition to smart manufacturing demands new skills from workers at all levels, from shop floor operators to senior management. Organizations that invest in comprehensive training programs and change management initiatives see higher adoption rates and better performance outcomes.

The logistics industry has undergone perhaps the most visible digital transformation, with technology reshaping every aspect of how goods move from point A to point B. Modern logistics providers leverage a combination of real-time tracking, route optimization, and predictive analytics to achieve unprecedented levels of efficiency and service quality.

Consider how last-mile delivery has evolved: AI-powered systems now optimize delivery routes in real-time, accounting for traffic patterns, weather conditions, and changing customer preferences. Mobile applications provide customers with minute-by-minute tracking updates, while automated warehouses use robots to pick and pack orders with remarkable speed and accuracy.

The impact of these technologies on performance has been substantial. Leading logistics providers report:

- 30-40% reduction in delivery times

- 20-25% decrease in operating costs

- 50% improvement in resource utilization

- 15-20% reduction in carbon emissions

These improvements stem from the intelligent integration of multiple technologies. GPS tracking systems work in concert with IoT sensors to provide real-time visibility into shipment locations and conditions. AI-powered planning systems optimize routes and resource allocation, while automated warehouses ensure efficient order fulfillment.

8.3 Retail's Customer-Centric Innovation

The retail sector has pioneered customer-centric supply chain solutions, driven by the need to meet increasingly demanding consumer expectations. The rise of omnichannel retail has forced companies to reimagine their supply chains from the ground up, creating seamless integration between online and offline channels.

Modern retail supply chains employ sophisticated demand forecasting systems that combine historical sales data with external factors like weather patterns, social media trends, and local events to predict customer demand with remarkable accuracy. This enhanced forecasting capability enables retailers to optimize inventory levels across their networks, reducing both stockouts and excess inventory.

Blockchain technology has emerged as a powerful tool for enhancing supply chain transparency in retail. Leading retailers use blockchain to track products from source to shelf, providing customers with detailed information about product origins, manufacturing conditions, and transportation history. This transparency not only builds customer trust but also enables better quality control and faster response to potential issues.

As we look toward the future, several emerging technologies promise to further revolutionize supply chain operations:

Quantum Computing

Quantum computing stands poised to transform supply chain optimization. While still in its early stages, quantum computers' ability to process complex calculations exponentially faster than classical computers could revolutionize everything from route optimization to inventory management. Early experiments suggest that quantum computing could solve certain supply chain optimization problems in minutes that currently take traditional computers days or weeks to process.

Advanced AI and Machine Learning

The next generation of AI systems will move beyond simple automation to true cognitive capabilities. These systems will be able to:

- Autonomously identify and respond to supply chain disruptions

- Predict and prevent potential issues before they occur

- Optimize operations across multiple objectives simultaneously

- Learn and adapt from experience in real-time

5G and 6G Networks

The rollout of 5G networks, and the future promise of 6G, will enable new levels of connectivity and real-time operation in supply chains. These high-speed, low-latency networks will support:

- Real-time coordination between autonomous systems

- Enhanced video analytics and quality control

- Augmented reality applications for warehouse operations

- Seamless integration of edge computing devices

Extended Reality (XR)

The convergence of virtual, augmented, and mixed reality technologies is creating new possibilities for supply chain operations. Applications include:

- Virtual training environments for complex operations

- Augmented reality guidance for maintenance and repair

- Virtual design and simulation of supply chain networks

- Enhanced visualization of data and analytics

8.5 Preparing for the Future

As these technologies continue to evolve, organizations must prepare themselves for the future of digital supply chains. This preparation requires attention to several key areas:

Infrastructure Development

Organizations need to develop flexible, scalable technology infrastructure that can accommodate new capabilities as they emerge. This infrastructure must support:

- High-speed data processing and analysis

- Secure integration of multiple systems and partners

- Real-time operation and decision-making

- Adaptive learning and optimization

Workforce Development

The future supply chain workforce will need new skills and capabilities. Organizations must invest in:

- Technical training and certification programs

- Digital literacy and data analysis skills

- Change management and adaptation capabilities

- Continuous learning and development programs

Process Innovation

Organizations must reimagine their processes to take full advantage of new technologies. This includes:

- Redesigning workflows for automation and optimization

- Developing new approaches to decision-making

- Creating more flexible and adaptive operations

- Integrating sustainability into core processes

Conclusion

The future of digital supply chains promises unprecedented levels of efficiency, transparency, and responsiveness. Success in this evolving landscape will require organizations to balance technological innovation with practical implementation considerations. Those that can effectively navigate this transformation while maintaining focus on value creation and sustainable growth will be best positioned to thrive in the digital future.

As we move forward, the key to success lies not just in adopting new technologies, but in creating integrated, adaptive systems that can evolve with changing business needs. Organizations must maintain a careful balance between innovation and stability, ensuring that their digital transformation efforts create lasting value while managing risks and resources effectively.

The journey toward fully digital supply chains continues to evolve, driven by technological advancement and changing market demands. By understanding current trends and preparing for future developments, organizations can position themselves to take advantage of new opportunities while building resilient, sustainable operations for the future.

www.ingramcontent.com/pod-product-compliance
Lightning Source LLC
LaVergne TN
LVHW081807050326
832903LV00027B/2128

*9 7 9 8 3 1 1 8 3 3 7 5 2 *